*Progress of*
*Another Pilgrim*

# Books by Frances J. Roberts

## Come Away, My Beloved
*This book will help you find the quiet place of communion, sense the presence of God and respond to His overtures. A six-part compilation of the six booklets listed below.*

*Lovest Thou Me?*      *Learn to Reign*
*Living Water*      *Listen to the Silence*
*Launch Out!*      *The Sounding of the Trumpet*

## Total Love
*A companion book to "Come Away, My Beloved." Fresh food for the soul. Encouraging, Holy Spirit-anointed. Pertinent message for today's challenges.*

## Dialogues with God
*Devotional writings. Similar to "Come Away, My Beloved."*

## Make Haste, My Beloved
*A tender but insistent call from the heart of God to the heart of His people. It is a call to purity: a light illuminating our path. A book you will read today and keep forever.*

## On the Highroad of Surrender
*A choice spiritual feast awaits you in this book which plumbs the depths and scales the heights of divine revelation. Inspiring and practical.*

## Progress of Another Pilgrim
*Challenging, inspirational. A thrilling sequel to "Come Away, My Beloved" and "Dialogues with God."*

## When the Latch Is Lifted
*A delightful gift book of heartwarming poetry. Illustrated. (This was listed in Total Love)*

## Angel in the Fire
*A beautiful book on death, grief and eternal life. Gift quality, with four full page pictorial illustrations.*

## Christmas Reflections
*A compilation of Frances J. Roberts' writings, poems and songs on the Advent theme. Parchment. Illustrated. Gift book.*

## O Wondrous Love
*A long-play stereo record of ten beautiful songs with words and music by Frances J. Roberts.*

Published by KING'S FARSPAN, INC.
1473 S. La Luna Ave., Ojai, California 93023

# PROGRESS
# OF ANOTHER
# PILGRIM

Frances J. Roberts

Cover photo by Steven Dibblee.

# Contents

In memory of my father
LEONARD H. JOHNSTON

Who led me to Christ at an early age,
and whose saintly life created an atmosphere
that made it natural to know and love God.

# Serenity and vitality

*Beside the still waters, let our souls find refreshing. In quiet meditation let our minds be renewed. For out of much concourse in the world there comes a fatigue of body which sleep alone cannot relieve. Out of solitude is born serenity, and out of serenity is born the vitality to meet the demands of life in every area of experience.*

*The life of God is imparted to man as he worships. Nothing so unfits the soul for the stresses of life as neglecting this solemn and joyous occupation. To be fully occupied with God the first hour of the day energizes the life forces and creates the capacity to meet the emergencies of any day, however trying.*

*Many a crisis loses its force when met by one who has gained poise and inner calm at the outset of the day.*

*The Psalmist, David, called the Lord his SHEPHERD because he had learned the secret of following. No path is too rugged if He has gone before. No place is desolate in His company. And so we journey . . . not in self-sufficiency and worldly wisdom, but in the way He leads: thus shall we be assured that we will not lose our way, and we shall have the added comfort of never having to walk alone.*

*Blessed Shepherd, guard and keep us.*

*Let Thy wisdom be our guide.*

*By the pools of grace and patience*

*Let us evermore abide.*

*We adore Thee, blessed Saviour;*

*Never let us turn from Thee.*

*Discipline our souls in kindness,*

*Tune our hearts to worship Thee.*

# Orientation of soul

It is not by the energy of the flesh that you enter into the kingdom. It is by much endurance in testings and tribulations that I teach and guide you into new paths.

My heart is a sanctuary, and as you pray I would bring you into oneness with Me in worship. This is a holy place, and sin must be purged away before you can enter with joy. Do not attempt to enter this place before you have humbled yourself and laid aside all self-esteem and self-seeking.

I have much work to be done, but I cannot use any vessel that is not fully surrendered to Me in total dedication. Your orientation of soul must be centered in Me. If you are out of balance and centered in your own self, you will always minister to the destruction of both yourself and others. This is why you must never enter upon service for Me prompted by self-will. It will always work toward disaster and confusion.

# Only yield the vessel

Be obedient to the still small voice. It will call you aside. It will engage your soul in devotion. It will give you direction, but first and of most importance, it will revive and enlighten your own spirit and imbue your soul with divine love.

I am in your midst, dwelling deep within your being. You need not search for Me any further away than your own heart. I have come to reside there by your own invitation. Do not turn outward again and ignore Me, but look in and know that what I give you to share with others will very truly be not ministering of yourself, but the flowing forth of My Spirit from His abiding place within you.

He shall move through you and speak through you, and you shall marvel at that which He shall do. Only yield your vessel. He is your victory.

Romans 8:14

# Look deeply

My child, look deeply within your heart, and much will be revealed. You are dull of hearing, having heard so much. I have other ways of dealing. Many things will become clear to you as you look into your innermost being. It is a storehouse of wisdom. Fear it not, for it is a deep pool of divine life because I Myself reside there.

I will teach you in symbols as you learn to see in the Spirit. You shall discover many treasures that have been stored and forgotten and lie waiting to be reclaimed.

Dismiss traditions. You disdain them but you still allow yourself to be held in bondage to them. Drive out the bondman. The slave shall not inherit with the free-born. Your spirit needs free course for expression. Do not hamper it in ignorance.

Gal. 1:11-16

# Fellowship

The night is dark and growing darker. This is why you must not go alone. This is why you have need to stand together, to pray together, to encourage each other and to be in communication with those like-minded. You need to be in contact with as many as possible of these, My "peculiar people." Think not that you are overextending yourself. You have not even begun to enter into what I have for you by way of associations and Holy Spirit fellowship.

Be not hindered. You are being held by nothing more than the usual — the familiar, the humdrum schedule. Break out of it as I direct. Let it not imprison you, for I have much work for you to do in other pastures. MOVE, and I will order your steps as you go, and I will give you a rich ministry.

Col. 3:12-17

# Integrity a sacred charge

There is a way that you must go because of faithfulness to Me. All you do, let it be as unto Me. Never do anything as pleasing men, but do all for Me and for My glory. Thus, and only thus, can your heart be kept at peace, and only in this way can you honor Me and bring forth fruit.

My Name is as perfume. Let it ever be upon your lips. Speak of Me often, and all other relationships shall be hallowed.

The integrity of your own heart is your most sacred charge. Guard this with utmost care.

I Cor. 10:31

# Project blessing

Borrow nothing of tomorrow's trouble. By anticipating evil you may create the same. Project blessing, and blessing will come to you.

Leave every anxiety at the foot of the cross. I have not exhausted My resources in helping you. Your faith is flagging. Back to the Word and strengthen your soul with heavenly manna.

I will keep you and bless you, and you shall bear My words of comfort to others.

Matt. 6:34a

# The simplicity of obedience

You need not search for answers to the many mysteries of life, but only trust and follow Me in the simplicity of obedience. Understanding will come to you as you walk in obedience.

Make Me your goal, and wisdom shall be given each day as needed. Do not try to reverse the order.

Job 28:28

# Hidden resources

There is no alternative for faith. You have need of testings to develop your character. There is no other way. Avoidance of stress genders weakness. Accept the trials of life as they come, and look for the good in each. Only in this way can you advance and grow in stature.

Only through much self-discipline and self-denial can you gain the victory. Undergirding you are My promises, and in them you shall find strength. Look not within yourself, for of yourself you can bring forth no goodness.

It is only through the power of My Spirit within you that you shall be able to tap hidden resources that have power to sustain you above yourself. Therefore you are not dependent upon nor limited by the level of your own strength of character, but you may rise above it and lift your own actions up into My divine pattern for you. This you can accomplish simply by relying more fully upon My help.

Rom. 5:3-5

# Your heart, a rebel

You have been acting as though you supposed you had to stand alone, in your own strength. You have experienced My help in innumerable places and situations. Why should you think that now, in this place, you must stand alone? No, you can never stand alone anywhere. You cannot solve any problem while you hold it in your own hands. Commit it to Me.

Commit THIS to Me. COMMIT it to ME. It is the only way. Your thoughts will deceive you, and your heart is a rebel. Fears assail and doubts plague you. Only surrender can take you out of the fiery furnace and put you back into My divine will so that I can give you peace again, and joy.

Psalm 37:5

# Union of spirit

There is a flow of divine life, and as you enter into it, you shall find victory. If you long to see your own personal wishes subjugated to the will and purposes of God, let your heart be at rest. For this union of your spirit with My Spirit and of your will and My will shall come as simply and easily as rain falling, if you can learn this one secret, that is, how to lose yourself in the flow of My life as I live within you.

John 17:23

# Seek Me in the hidden places

Understanding comes not by outer observation but by inner revelation. I Myself will teach you. I Myself will open to you many mysteries. Fret not, neither set a limit as to what you may attain. I will communicate with you more and more, and at a deeper level of understanding, as you seek Me in the hidden places of your soul.

I Cor. 2:10-14

# Repentance activates My grace

*Give Me all*: your body, mind and spirit. Hold nothing back for yourself. Speak to Me often and much. The more you do so, the more I can help you. Full confession brings full forgiveness. True humility opens the door to divine aid. Genuine repentance activates My grace.

I John 1:9, 10

# Perfecting of soul

If you set up barriers through pride or self-defense, you hinder the progress of your soul. Be as a little child, and stay open to the flow of My life in you: so shall you be spared many a bitter disappointment and much weary striving. Only in this way can you keep your balance and poise. Thus shall your perfecting be accomplished.

Nothing you could ever do for Me can be more important than this — the perfecting of your own soul.

Heb. 13:20, 21

# An injection of new life

All you do for Me in ministering to others is part of My own working within you; for in every case, whenever you bless another, you bring an injection of new life and vitality into your own spirit and personality.

Your character is that which I shape from the broken fragments of all your testings; therefore, accept the trials with a grateful heart. I will use ALL things to bring you into conformity to My image if you will but bless all and trust Me.

I Peter 1:5-9

# The tranquility of worship

There is a way of the Spirit unknown to the natural mind. No barrier can keep you from finding His best for you except an unyielding will. As long as it is your sincere desire to know and to do the will of God, He will guide and direct you in all sorts of surprising ways.

His desire to bless you goes infinitely beyond your own personal effort to secure His blessing.

There is always peace in His presence. Do not disturb this by anxiety about what is in store for tomorrow. Out of the very tranquility of worship shall be born the guidance you need.

Matt. 6:33, 34

# His grace is activated by your desire

Give Him your full adoration. His grace toward you extends through the channel of your love, and is activated by your desire to receive.

Enter upon each day with the quiet knowing: Christ is in this day because Christ is in Me.

You can go nowhere without finding Him, because wherever you go, you take Him with you, and He goes before and follows after.

Psalm 23

# Give Me every heartache

My child, know that I am guiding and leading. Nothing can be amiss as long as your heart is right with Me. I am in full control of all that touches your life when you are in tune with Me.

Lay every care at My feet. Give Me every heartache and every concern. I will make your way clear, so that you will not stumble nor be turned to a false way.

There has been no time when you have needed Me as deeply as you need Me now.

Psalm 37:23

# Riches at your feet

My ways are not your ways. My perfect timing seems slow to you because of your spirit of impatience. Some of My most precious gifts are unrecognized by you because of your blind ingratitude. Many a lovely experience can come to you and not be received because of your insensitivity at that particular moment.

Angels have knocked at your door and been turned away as beggars because you were dull of perception. Could the truth be revealed, you would view with awe and astonishment the untold riches that have been heaped at your feet and have been stepped over as though an obstacle when they might have been gathered and used to open other doors of fulfillment, yes, of ministry.

The past you cannot change, but TODAY IS YOURS. Live it to the fullest of your awakened awareness. Don't miss an opportunity to turn every moment "inside out" . . . to reveal the hidden glory, the potential with which I have invested it.

This is truly the secret of manifesting My life. This is precisely what I did Myself in the days of My ministry on earth. In every place and in every association with people, I simply let shine forth My eternal glory. You may do the same, as you let ME live in and through you.

It is so simple. It is MY way. Having sincerely tried it, you will not be satisfied to live any other way.

Gen. 28:16

# Chastening

No chastening is pleasant, but you need it for your growth in the graces of the Spirit. Move ahead in confidence in spite of every obstacle.

Mine eye is upon you.

Heb. 5:8; 12:5, 6

# Strivings hinder

My people are drifting like a boat with empty sails. But I shall blow, saith the Lord; yes, I shall cause a mighty wind to rise, and the sails shall be filled, and the Spirit shall drive you forward. You shall rejoice in Me and praise My Name.

In your own power you can accomplish nothing whatsoever in the kingdom of God. I need your submission, but I do not need your help.

All strivings only hinder. Love is the only telling contribution you can make toward the perfecting of your soul.

John 14:23

# Drink deeply of My love

Be silent, My little one. My peace shall come to you as you think about Me and as you open to Me your heart. Be not disturbed by what you feel, but set your thoughts on what you know and what I have revealed to you, and new faith shall spring forth.

Never doubt My love when things are dark. Situations never change Me. The deeper your need, the more I will respond if you call on Me. In this way you can turn the darkness into blessing.

Hold to My hand. No other support is necessary. Human love is comforting, but divine love, the love of God the Father, is greater. I desire to give you both, but if you can drink deeply of My love, you shall come more quickly to find fulfillment in human love also.

As you reach out, reach out to Me alone. I will never fail to meet you when your desire for Me is pure and sincere. I know your every heartache and see each falling tear. I will gather you to My heart and you shall know the deep, deep joy of being near Me.

Psalm 139:12

# Seek Me when the sun is shining

Give Me every care. Give Me every burden. Give Me every fear. I stand ready to help you. You have only BE-GUN to taste of My goodness. *I am loving you all the time,* but you come to Me mostly in periods of stress. I want to teach you to live continually in My presence. I can give you more constructive help when you are well than when you are sick, but when you are well you are too busy to give Me the opportunity to minister.

So I help you now in the hour of discouragement, and I ask you to seek Me when the sun is shining and all is well again. Now I can comfort: then I can teach. Now I can bless you, but then I can help you even more.

Be obedient. I have a beautiful work for you to do for Me.

Psalm 55:22


# The beauty of silence

Lay your head in silence upon My bosom. Speaking is for later. Learning will evolve out of communion in due time, but do not try to mix the two. You are ofttimes over-anxious to learn. I rejoice in your desire to understand, but you shall see Me most clearly in a silent pool. Words are as pebbles which when dropped into quiet water send out ripples and distort the image. I shall minister to you in the beauty of the silence in ways that I could never communicate by words. Let Me look deep into your soul, and as I search you out and know you, I shall bless you in a mysterious way.

Psalm 139:17, 18

# Tribulation and stamina

Only through much prayer can you endure much tribulation. In no other way can the new life in Christ develop and gain stamina.

Be as a child and trust your Father implicitly. He will honor your faith and will give you still more.

Do not place restrictions on divine aid by trying to live the Christian life in your own strength. Christ Himself is your victory. His kingdom shall be forever, but even now it is in your heart whenever you bow to Him as sovereign.

Col. 1:27

# Testings

In a multitude of testings I would perfect your understanding. I am not unaware of the pressures thus inflicted upon you, but as the trials come and go, I not only turn them into a means of blessing, but I never fail to make available My comfort and My sustaining strength.

I Peter 1:7

# Crisis experiences

I will never leave you alone in the midst of any affliction. You cannot escape the crisis experiences if you desire to grow and mature, but you need never fear them regardless of the form they take, for My grace and My equanimity shall be as a strong anchor that shall hold you fast, and you shall not be driven off course.

I Peter 5:10

# Accept it as from Me

Do not wait until calamity strikes to prepare your soul. The inner fortification which you shall need must be built up in advance. Men do not walk onto a battlefield and win a victory, nor even survive, without preparation.

I have called you apart and made provision for your spiritual and physical needs. Take full advantage of this and do not in any way deplete your strength. You need all the care obtainable at this time. Do not consider it a luxury. I have given it, and I would have you accept it as from Me. This will free you of an undue sense of obligation to the one I have seen fit to make available as a channel to bless you and will give you the proper spirit of gratitude that will be as a spiritual gift to the other person.

Psalm 23:5

# Preparation

No event in your life is a mistake. I will use every circumstance to enrich your ministry and perfect your soul. You have seen only the beginning. It is I who have set the world in your heart. All you feel of world concern is by My Spirit. You shall go because I have need of you, and you shall minister in the full power of your calling.

You shall go not by man's bidding, but I shall thrust you forth. Be not surprised, neither question how it shall come to pass. The opening of doors is My responsibility; but the preparation of your soul is your own responsibility.

Do not fail. If you would be ready when the time comes, you must be diligent now and follow My guidance in every detail with the greatest care. You are not pampering the flesh but strengthening the body that it may be an adequate vehicle to carry the Spirit.

Isaiah 48:17

# Singleness of heart

By singleness of heart you will escape much of the complexities that generate confusion and anxiety. Keep your mind at rest, and let worship be your supreme occupation. This you can never overdo.

Seek My face, and seek My counsel: but as you do so, bring Me first your love, and as you experience My help in daily living, come back again to Me with your gratitude and praise.

*I do not ask of you great achievements, but great devotion.* I do not require lavish gifts, but I am jealous of your praise.

Psalm 51:15, 16

# Seek My wisdom

I will give you strength unlimited as long as you do that which you know to be right. Your faith shall be strong and your needs met: only take your directions from Me and listen closely for My guidance.

Do not react to the stimuli around you, but seek My wisdom carefully. I will give you the word of knowledge and all your steps shall be ordered by Me.

Be diligent and be faithful, and your satisfaction shall come from Me. Your path shall be strewn with blessing, and My eternal kingdom shall be furthered. Wherever you go, know that you take Me with you, and I will perfect all that concerneth you.

Underneath are the everlasting arms. Rest upon them. Your strength shall not fail, for I shall be your support. No evil tidings shall bring distress if you remember that your times are in My hand.

Psalm 37:5

# True dedication

The Lord is calling you aside into a walk of Faith. There is no self-denial possible without full surrender. There are forms of self-punishment that cloak themselves in the robes of dedication but are really false expressions and not true piety. Only God can lay upon you a true spirit of humility and dedication. Only His love can motivate a genuine self-sacrifice.

Do not deceive yourself. Let Him try your motives and probe the depths of your heart. Only He knows your true desire, and only He is able to purify your desire and deepen your commitment.

His eye is upon you. His intention is to bless you, not to cause you unnecessary suffering. His hand chastens, but His love comforts.

Go your way in peace, knowing He has promised to perfect that which concerneth you, and His ways are ways of wisdom.

I Cor. 11:32

# Fight discouragement

My son, turn not from the path of truth. Many testings shall beset you, but your God shall be your refuge. He shall undergird you, and send His holy angels to keep watch over you, and you shall not be afraid regardless of the hazards.

Open wide your soul, and the Lord will fill it with His goodness. Your heart shall drink in His mercy and love; for His ear is attuned to your cry, and your desire toward Him shall be generously rewarded.

He knows your need and the depth of your searching. Only as you fight discouragement can you make room for Him to bless you in full measure as He desires to do.

Col. 3:1-4

# Faith, a perpendicular operation

Be alert. Keep your thoughts always on Me. Give Me your trouble, WHATEVER it may be. There is no disturbance big enough to warrant your distress, because ANYTHING committed to Me will be taken care of.

Be steadfast, and be one about whom it can be said that you truly live and walk BY FAITH. I will be with you and help you, and I will be your strength.

No barrier shall stand in your way, because faith is a perpendicular operation. Your faith reaches straight up to Me, and My power comes straight down upon the place of action.

Be obedient to the gentlest promptings of My Spirit, for in a time of crisis you are subject to more than the normal amount of distraction.

Rom. 14:23

# Break old patterns

The time is *now* because the hour is late; yes, there is not a *day* left, but an *hour*. There is not time for incidentals because of the sheer urgency. Run after Me as I move, because I am moving rapidly and am doing a quick work. Pay no attention to any voice except the voice of the Spirit. Let no one use you except the Father. Believe no one except the Son. Live in expectancy and move in absolute obedience.

Break out of old patterns, and make no provision for your own personal wishes. Purify your desires so that you do not stand in your own way.

Matt. 8:22

# Thy healing touch

Father, I need Thy help. When my heart cries after Thee in willingness to sacrifice, my body resists because of weariness or pain. Let me know Thy healing touch as I move with Thee. Let my body be invigorated by the power of Thy Spirit, otherwise it detains and rebels when needed most to serve.

Let me not recognize my physical limitations as a potential handicap, but increase my faith so that I may simply assume that when a work is to be done, the strength will be provided by Thee, that I may no longer pamper the flesh, making provision for its weakness.

Psalm 18:32

# The armour of light

O My child, I call you to surrender. No problem confronts you that I cannot resolve. Given the opportunity, I will spare you disappointment and regret. You have acted on impulse and curiosity rather than waiting for clear guidance. Confess, and I will forgive, and I will extricate you from this situation that you have brought upon yourself.

You ran ahead of Me and fell into a snare. I will go with you Myself and make the crooked places straight and we will go on again, TOGETHER. This time you will wait for My leading and not take the initiative. Let this teach you the lesson that you are ALWAYS in danger when you move out on your own.

Wear the armour of the Spirit, and you have My protection. Fear not what others can do to harm you. Fear only your own tendency to act independently. Every transaction is important to Me, so do not feel that I am ever a disinterested party.

Jer. 10:23

## I am everywhere

Never flounder on the rocks of indecision. The call of My heart to you is for your utter abandon to the waters of My will. I AM EVERYWHERE. Think not that any man can shut Me out. Wherever you go you bear the Wind of the Spirit. It shall bring new life into any situation. It shall breathe upon the dead, and they shall live. It shall touch the one who has completely given up with a ray of new courage, so that though he may have lost all hope he shall be lifted out of the place of despondency into My loving arms and into an atmosphere of faith once again.

Matt. 10:8

## By divine appointment

Go *anywhere* that you are led by Me. Go as many places as time allows. You pass this way by My divine appointment. You pass alone because I have made you free to do My bidding without being hampered by others.

Always make your ministry your FIRST responsibility. Others may be surprised, as were Mary and Joseph when Jesus was detained unduly in the temple, but they shall not stand in the way, for I have planned your way and strewn it with jewels.

I shall be your strength. I shall be your grace. I shall be your wisdom. You shall do valiantly because your expectation is from the Lord.

Psalm 32:8

# Listen carefully

The time is short. Listen carefully to My words. Hide them in your heart; for they need a time for developing within you, even as seeds that are planted in the earth. My word needs a period to rest quietly within your heart until it is quickened by the Spirit. Then shall it rise in newness of life. In this way I will bring forth through you new truth and fresh revelation.

# Pools of reflection

No new truth can be generated in the midst of activity. New life springs from the placid pools of reflection. Quiet meditation and deep worship are a prerequisite if you are to receive My words and comprehend My thoughts.

Some graces of the soul are gained in motion. Faith may be developed in action; endurance in the midst of storms and turmoil. Courage may come in the front lines of battle. But wisdom and understanding and revelation unfold as dew forms on the petals of a rose — in quietness.

Did not Jesus learn from His Father through the silences of lonely nights on the mountain? Shall I not teach you likewise? Will you, My child, set aside unto Me these hours for lonely vigil that I may have opportunity to minister to you?

# Examine your way

Do you hear the voice that calls you? Will you stop and ponder and listen to Me as I speak to you? Know you not that I love you? Why would you avoid a confrontation? I am not angry with you. You are disturbed with yourself.

You have come into a place of consternation because you have neglected the place of solitude and communion.

I have intentionally let you feel many distressing things in order to cause you to examine your way. It will not be hard to find the path of peace whenever you are prepared to pay the price to walk in it. To find it any sooner would be of no help!

Isa 54:7-10

## My ordained will

I lead those who delight in My way. I need you on this path . . . the path of My ordained will for you. Friends may bless and help, but only I can bring you into full victory.

You find it, and you lose it. I would help you in such a way that you will be able to find it and remain in it. I cannot do anything for you as long as you go on in self-determination. The joy of victory is so wonderful that it is cheap at any price. I want you to have it, and I know, even when you doubt, that you are willing to pay it.

Psalm 37:23

## I require more

Strive to be perfectly yielded to the Holy Spirit. He will do much for you BEYOND what has been done in you up to this point. You have truly given ME much in the past, but I require MORE now because of the ministry I have for you to accomplish.

Let Me work in you with full liberty. You cannot do it yourself. *I am the sanctifier.* Only give Me the freedom to work. You will be amazed at how easily it can be done.

I Thess. 5:23, 24

# The fruits of the Spirit

My little children, I would speak to you concerning the fruits of the Spirit. I would have you understand how My presence within you, My divine life operating in your human heart, creates the fruits of the Spirit.

It is not by self-effort that these heavenly attributes are brought forth. Verily the fruits of the Spirit are not native to the world. The carnal man never brings forth this fruit. He may at times produce something that seems to be similar, but it will always be a substitute unacceptable to Me.

*Love, joy and peace*: these were natural to Jesus, but they are foreign to man's fallen nature. You will never produce them by seeking to suppress evil emotions. I am able to bring them forth even from your inmost being as you allow Me to LIVE in you.

Gal. 5:22, 23

# The Father's husbandry

*Faith, meekness, temperance*: these are fruits that mature slowly, and they are perfected by the careful husbandry of the Father. There is a kind of faith that is a gift of God. This is believing faith for initial salvation. The faith which is produced within you as fruit of the Holy Spirit is a faith operating in the life of the believer to the end that he becomes a productive vehicle for the doing of the Father's work. Yes, and this fruit of meekness goes beyond mildness of temperament, even to an acceptance of injustice. It is not only patient, but gracious — returning good for evil. This is verily a divine fruit. This you may experience as you yield fully to My Spirit within.

And the ultimate goodness, the *summum bonum* of all, is temperance. Because of the lack of this particular fruit many an otherwise vigorous Christian has found himself cut down at the roots (Phil. 4:5)

John 15:1

# Spiritual awareness

As a child has eyesight, but only by teaching and study does he learn the art of reading, so likewise, what I do for you is to train you to comprehend intelligently that which you see in the Spirit.

The same principle applies in the other areas of spiritual awareness. Know that you HAVE five avenues of spiritual operation, and let Me be your teacher and guide you into how to interpret the information that comes to you in these various ways.

It is I who have given these faculties. Know that as you serve Me you shall have very definite need of the information I will give through these avenues. It will provide you with a knowledge of dangers and will give you insight into the needs of people to whom you minister. I will make your words meaningful to the individual and your heart sensitive to his needs.

I Cor. 2:12-14


# Critical missions

Apply yourself to learning, for I have need of you as a master workman. I am assigning you to critical missions, and lives are at stake. Mistake not My voice, for much evil is being unleashed upon the earth, and man's need is becoming more and more desperate.

Do not fail Me. I will NEVER fail you. I will shield you and protect you and I will heal every wound. I will be a never-failing source of comfort and help, and My Spirit will be so strong in you that you shall not be dependent upon your vacillating physical energy. Your very body shall be energized and propelled by My Spirit, and I will not let you faint in the way.

Psalm 27:11

# The soul is directional

My people need direction. There are many pressures which influence them, but they need to hear a clear voice giving them the wisdom of God. When their state of being is profitless insofar as the work of My kingdom is concerned, it is due to their inability to hear My voice, in whatever form it may come to them. No man shall find himself in such a state except by his own choice, be that conscious or otherwise.

The soul is directional, and any heart turned toward Me in an attitude of true worship shall receive from Me a quickening flow of life. It cannot be otherwise.

Those who do not hear Me are occupying themselves with other thoughts. They may even be studying the Bible and fail to hear My voice speaking to their heart, but they cannot WORSHIP Me and miss Me.

I am eager to meet all and every one who comes to sit at My feet and be taught in the Spirit.

Luke 10:38-42


# Be not negligent

Be not negligent concerning the gift I have given you. Do not allow it to become dormant. I have given it to you knowing full well the urgency of this hour. Be up and about your Father's business. Let nothing else claim priority over this, My commission to you.

You shall suffer loss, and not you alone but multitudes of others, if indolence overtakes you. My people are searching for food, and the pastures are sparse. There is need for the provision of nourishment. Yes, My Body must be fed and cared for and supplied the necessary nutriments for health and growth.

II Tim. 1:6-14

# Give yourself to prayer and the Word

Give yourself to a life of prayer and much careful study of the Word, that you may be able to give My message with clarity and the unction of the Holy Spirit.

Reduce your activities and dispose of non-essentials. Concentrate your thoughts and intentions upon Jesus Christ, and in Him seek your wisdom and comfort. I will open avenues to aid you, for this is My will for you, and you can know that I will always make a way for the performance of My will in your life once you have set your goal to be obedient to My commands. Is it not written that I give you the desires of your heart? Give yourself to the desire, and I shall give Myself to the fulfillment.

Acts 6:4

# The seeds of the Word

Lo, the message is Mine, but I have need of those who will speak it and those who will give it faithfully without alteration and without any attempt to please men.

I have much to say that is not pleasant to hear, because the heart of man has grown fat with self-interest, and the light of the knowledge of the things of God has grown dim. Many walk in darkness, not hearing the call to repentance.

The seeds of the Word have long since dried up and died in many a prayerless life. I need those who will speak it again and send it out afresh in the dynamic power of the Holy Spirit. This is what brings conviction and regeneration. The Word must be spoken through those who are themselves spiritually alive, otherwise in passing through the vessel it loses its power to produce new life.

Isaiah 6

# Exalt His Name

Let none tell you He is as others . . . lo, He is the Son of God, yes, He is God the Son. Exalt His Name and rejoice in His majesty; for the heavens were fashioned by His hand, and man is His creation. What man of all earth's personages can lay claim to any such power of creation?

Yes, His works alone shall proclaim His power and deity. Man cannot extinguish the light of His glorious works.

John 1:1, 2

# Humility and compassion

O My precious little one, you can never know how very dear you are to My heart. I can safely tell you how deeply I love you, because knowing the extent of My love for you can only make your heart more tender. Knowing My love never generates pride. On the contrary, it causes a humility incomparably sweet and precious. Humility of this kind is never produced simply by ridding the soul of pride. Rather, it is a humility blended with tenderness and compassion, because it is a response to My divine love and thus reflects the gentleness of My own heart. It is a quality of spirit which invades the inmost soul, but although it would seem to be hidden like a precious treasure in your innermost being, lo, in truth it can never be concealed, for the light of it and the glory of it radiates from your entire countenance.

This outer manifestation of My love I allow others to see as you minister, yes, as you look in compassion upon the needy soul. This is that which verily ministers to their hunger even before you speak a word. It is this reflection of My meek and lowly heart which awakens and calls forth a response, and in so doing allows you to make contact with the right ones and speak words to ears that I am opening.

Know that as you receive My love and as your soul is saturated with My divine compassion and grace, your ministry is enhanced and your own hunger satisfied.

# Recognize My hand

Surely I have called you and led you by the hand and have brought you through a rough and stony way. You can look ahead and see the rolling pastures and a good and pleasant land. Know that My joy is for you, and I am with you in the place of blessing.

How often I have assured you that there would be a reward for your faithfulness. You are now at a place where you can already lift up your eyes and look upon it.

I have prepared this for you, and I have stood beside you through the times of endurance, and I have smiled, knowing what was in store for you. I have urged you on when you would have given up, because I would not allow you to fail.

Love Me more than ever. *Recognize My hand in this.* It is truly a divine appointment. You can accept it knowing I will be in it. Yes, I will bless and multiply it far beyond what you see now.

Have no fear. Your work is MY WORK, and I am well able to take care of every aspect.

II Sam. 22:20

# Take time out

My little one, lean heavily upon Me, and rest in the peace that I give you. No place on earth shall you find such comfort as leaning on My bosom, and at no time shall you know such complete release from all anxiety as when you are waiting in My presence.

My concern is for you, and I am mindful of every need. You have sacrificed of your time and strength in prayer and in service, and I say unto you, take time out to be still and to regather your forces and rebuild your vitality.

Matt. 11:28-30

# Health

You cannot labor on without respite. The power of the Spirit can immunize the body against attacks of weakness and disease, but you have still a responsibility to live in wisdom and take proper care of the body because it is a gift entrusted to you by God, and because you cannot serve Me effectively with an unhealthy, uncared-for body.

Health I would give in every area: body, soul and spirit. Work with Me in this, and it shall result in a more fruitful ministry.

Psalm 127:2

# Clothed in light

My child, no matter how dark the way may be, know that My life is power. In My presence all that has any part with the darkness shall be driven out.

As no man can know freedom who has not broken out of bondage, even so, none can stand clothed in light except he has been delivered out of all that is of the shadow.

Psalm 97:11

# Triumphs rise out of defeats

Be patient as My hand deals with you. Blessings are born out of pain. Triumphs rise out of the dust of defeats when the defeats are offered up to Me and you go on again in faith.

Never despair.

II Tim. 2:12

# Godly sorrow versus carnal

Overmuch sorrow causes the heart to fail. If you would be a rejoicing Christian, the griefs of the carnal man must be laid aside. There are sufferings of spirit through which every soul must pass in the process of perfection, but these are not to be compared to the complaints laid upon the soul which are directly related to uncrucified affections.

To bemoan any unpleasant natural circumstance accomplishes nothing but a heaping up of misery. Undue distress about untoward happenings is devastating to the soul. The only kind of sorrow that I can use for your good is the godly sorrow of true repentance.

Turn to Me in every trial, and give it all to Me.

Prov. 15:13

# Fortify your soul

Overcoming temptation involves more than your will, My child. It requires more than your desire to be holy, however sincere that may be. You do not possess the strength to overpower the adversary, and it is he who generates within you the compulsion to sin.

Only as you fortify your soul through feasting on My Word and by much prayer can you hope to be victorious. The power of My Spirit moves through the written word making it health to the marrow of your spiritual bones, giving you divine energy and clarifying your vision. The more your soul is saturated with the scriptures, the easier it will become to experience the free flow of My nature infusing your daily expression. To act contrary to My will becomes more and more difficult to those who know and love My word.

Romans 13:14; Eph. 6:16

# The healing pool

Whenever you are in any kind of trouble, know that My Spirit in the midst is like the angel who stirred the Pool of Bethesda and made it a place of healing. Disturbances which give every appearance of being natural become infused with divine purposes if your soul is allowed to lie in My hand.

You need not discern every experience in order to receive a blessing. I Myself touch circumstances and add the power of the miraculous, and you shall many times be startled to discover the reflection of My face in a very ordinary "pool".

John 5:2-4

# Anticipate Me everywhere

It has become customary for men to look for Me in cathedrals and in other places of quiet and beauty. Do not forget that I was found by Jacob in the country place, by Bartimaeus along a dusty road, and by Peter on the shore of the lake. Indeed, there is scarcely a place you can mention, nor a circumstance of life where it is not recorded that I have encountered man.

Look for Me, then, at all times and in all places, and in every kind of circumstance. I shall cross your path like flashes of sunlight breaking through forest trees.

Your life shall take on new meaning, and anticipation shall be your companion. Your every care shall be lightened, and your every sorrow healed.

My love shall enfold you, and My words shall give you strength. I will be your portion and your delight, and My joy shall be your salvation.

Psalm 139:7-12

# All is sacred

Be still, My child, and you shall hear My voice. It may be that because you fear what I say, you tune Me out. Come closer to Me. Everything I ever bring you is always for your blessing. It may be stern, or it may be tender, but always you shall thank Me for it because it will help you.

Too much activity is a heavy drain on your whole being. You are not three separate units: body, soul, and spirit. You are one unit, having three avenues of expression. When one part is unduly taxed, all are affected. Your soul can only be strong and rested as your body is also. Sleep shall bring refreshing and renewal to the spirit as much as to the body. Keep the image of yourself united, for it will benefit you much.

All is sacred, as all is dedicated for My glory. You do not glorify the flesh by giving proper care to physical needs. The only area in which I will not tolerate indulgence is in self-will. As long as your will is yielded to Me, all else will be simple.

# As a little child

Do not let others confuse you. Take what comes, and pass it on into My hands. I will apply whatever may be of value and discard the rest. I am dealing also with them through you, even though you are often unaware of this. If you knew in truth how I use your words, you would be hindered and would become a hindrance to Me.

Live as a little child. Truth is always simple. Love is unsophisticated. Holiness is uncluttered. Channels are undecorated. Don't make it difficult by asking so many questions.

# The forces of intercession

Bring the struggles within your soul to Me in prayer. It is the movement within you of the forces of intercession which you are feeling. It is not a personal struggle. The resolutions shall come as you pray, not as you search for wisdom as an end in itself.

Prayer has brought more illumination than books. Seek Me, and you shall KNOW. You shall understand more than you dream possible, and your inner peace shall deepen.

Rom. 8:26

# Physical health and spiritual ministry

Do not misconstrue the scripture which says "I beat my body to keep it in subjection". A more clear way to state the true intent would be to say, "By proper discipline and care of the physical body, it may be made to fulfill the desires and demands of the soul." Otherwise, you may by lack of concern for your physical health, hamper your spiritual ministry.

Run the race with a pure heart, and the reward shall be given you. Your path is strewn with blessings. Enjoy them fully and recognize that they are from My hand.

III John 1:2

# The Lord's day

This is *My* day, and you honor Me when you spend a sacred portion of it in My house. It matters not so much *where,* as *how.* If your heart is lifted up to Me and filled with love and adoration and gratitude, your soul shall receive ministry, and you will be used to minister to others.

Psalm 122, Heb. 10:25

# Angels are separating

Have I not spoken concerning the future day, that it shall be a day of the gathering of the wheat and of the destruction of the tares? Have I not said this work shall be done by angels? Behold, I say unto you that you have been witnessing a foretaste of this very thing. The wheat is being stored in the Father's granaries, and the tares are being bound in bundles, as it were, in preparation for the day of destruction.

You have been aware at times of the presence and ministry of angels. This is because this work, among others, is their responsibility. You, as believers, are being gathered unto the Father. Meanwhile those who are the children of wrath and disobedience are being separated from you and gathered to each other.

Truly, angels are separating. Know this when you would wonder why one is brought in and another goes out into the night, never to return. Question it not, for you are seeing this prophecy fulfilled, at least in part. It shall be accelerated as the end draws nearer.

You shall find in this understanding much peace of heart.

Matt. 13:39, 41, 49

# The importance of time and kindness

Time is of supreme importance. Waste none. Let Me help you know what is worthy of attention and what is not; otherwise you may be tempted to eliminate the things I most desire you to do.

Having a schedule will help you, but remember that kindness is more indicative of spiritual fervor than all your efficiency in work. Never let your works of righteousness crowd out the little acts of thoughtfulness. The labors of the hands must never take precedence over the gentle expressions of a compassionate heart.

Eph. 15:1, 2

# The motivation of love

Many a life could be simplified and enriched by doing less and loving more. Indeed, all that is ever done, if not motivated by divine love, is in vain. It is worse than doing nothing, for it is potentially destructive.

There are those who have risen to fame through their noble acts, only to fall into shame and disrepute because of a bitter spirit.

I Cor. 13:1

# There is always an alternative

No price is too great to pay for the proper care of that which I have given you. Never regard lightly that which is precious in My sight. There is always an alternative to the life of relinquishment, but it is lean and barren. That which is most precious needs to be offered up to Me continually.

My grace is as a beacon. It shall shed light on all that is now obscure.

Genesis 22:2

# A way of triumph

Never be led by human reasoning. The day is coming when you would have faltered but for the understanding I am giving you now.

It is a way of triumph when it leads to fuller enlightenment. When My presence is with you, you can know there is a blessing in store. It shall open to you as you trust Me. It shall be beautiful beyond your highest dreams.

I Cor. 2:9-16

# Why do you falter?

O My child, I have need of you. Have I not called you and blessed you? Have I not laid My hand upon you and shaped you for My purposes? Why, then, do you question, and why do you doubt?

It is only the patterns of the past that bind your thoughts. They can exert no power over tomorrow except as you deliberately give them life. With every task I assign, I also give the enablement. If I require something of you beyond what I have asked before, know that I intend to give you greater strength and clearer understanding, for I know full well that you are going to need it.

I have tested your faith many times, and I know it is strong. Why do you falter? Rise, and go in My Name, knowing it is I who thrust you forth. It is not man. This is *My* plan for you. The way should be easy when you know this.

Isa. 45:2, 3

# Communion

Communion with Me will purify the soul. Communion will motivate the prayer life. Communion will generate holy ardor. It will negate unworthy desires and block the pursuit of self-will.

Walking with Me is impossible to the disoriented soul, and you shall be so if you neglect communion.

To meditate is to find direction. You look outward in the world for guidance and information concerning natural things, but I say unto you, you must look INWARD to receive wisdom regarding matters of the Spirit.

Fail in anything else, if need be, but do not fail in this; for truly if you succeed in this, all else will be easy. You cannot fail in anything else in My sight when your life is blended with My life.

# Be responsive

Be responsive to the promptings of the Holy Spirit. I may not speak with a blast of the trumpet. It may be a touch on the shoulder. Do not wait for some climactic experience. Follow the still, small voice. Be obedient to the gentle moving of My Spirit. I often work this way because I want to develop your sensitivity.

I know your frailties, but in this way I purpose to make you strong. I know your hesitency, but by working with you in this quiet fashion, I would strengthen your faith. I know your cry for wisdom, and I am teaching you through each experience, even the most humble.

I Ki. 19:11, 12

# In shadow and sunshine

Rely upon Me in wholehearted trust. I am as much in the shadow as in the sunshine. Everywhere and in all circumstances My grace is in operation within you. Simply ALLOW it to work. You need not strive.

The work of the Spirit is as silent as white clouds moving across a blue sky. Do not make it complicated. I breathe across the heart-strings and bring forth melody. I put My words in your mouth and send them forth to create spiritual life.

Simply keep your soul-consciousness directed toward Me.

Psalm 34:1

# The realm of worship

Your one responsibility is to worship Me and lift other souls into this realm. Men have been taught all manner of things. I desire your worship above all else, and this is the most neglected.

Labor to live in the hallowed atmosphere of the holy place, and let your ministry to others be that of opening this door to them also. It is a glorious, sacred privilege. My blessing shall sanctify your life as you pursue this beautiful mission.

Psalm 100

# The spiritual senses

I have joined My soul unto your soul in a covenant of blood. I have redeemed you from destruction. I have refined you in the furnace of affliction. Now I will use you, and all I ask is that you stand before Me quietly and await the word from within. It will never fail. It will come forth with power just as the healing power comes forth when you move in faith and lay hands on the sick.

Did I not promise that I would send a rain of refreshing? I will surely fill your vessel with a mighty downpour of My reviving Spirit. I will quicken your senses and you shall *hear* in the Spirit, you shall *speak* in the Spirit, and you shall *discern* in the Spirit. You shall verily *feel* in the same way. For as man has five natural senses, regenerated souls have five spiritual senses, and every alert, healthy believer should have these operating.

The power is given you already. Exercise it and let Me educate you along these lines.

I Cor. 12:7-11

# Fulfillment

Every door that I open, you shall pass through. My Spirit shall speak, and you shall utter that which is given unto you.

You have been like a green plant. Now I would have you put forth blossoms. The flowering is a symbol of the manifestation of the Spirit. Yes, it is even more, it is fulfillment of original purpose. It is destiny. It is the ultimate end to which it was designated by the Creator. Anything less would be failure and disappointment.

Only to have life is not enough. Fulfillment is that for which I am waiting, yes, the manifestation of My sons and daughters as they come to maturity and as they produce that for which I created them.

John 15:8

# A door of utterance

Behold, I set before you a door of utterance. You shall open your mouth, and I will fill it. You shall go and not be detained. You shall glorify Me, and your own vessel shall be an open channel for the river of My grace.

You shall bring healing. You shall bring hope. You shall forget the former day when you had not strength to stand, for I shall uphold you and give you supernatural strength. I shall endue you with power from on high, and I shall magnify My word so that as you speak it forth I will confirm it, even with miracles following. Some of these may be spiritual miracles taking place in the hearts of those to whom you minister. Leave this to Me. Be faithful, and deliver My word, and I will surely bless it and cause it to be a creative word, a life-giving word, yes, a word of deliverance.

Mark 16:20

# Eternal values

Every motion in your life becomes impregnated with sublime significance as you are wholly dedicated to Me. All of time becomes charged with eternal values as it is consecrated and given to Me.

II Tim. 1:12

# Avoid frivolity

Avoid frivolity with the same carefulness as you disdain the grosser sins. The latter are transgressions of the law of God, but the former is a thief and will rob both yourself and others of spiritual good.

A bantering spirit may cause you to be oblivious to opportunities to minister that may lie directly in your path. Thus if you are indulging in spiritual profligacy, you rob the other person of the blessing you could have given, and you rob yourself of the reward you would have received had you been walking softly in the Spirit.

Matt. 12:36, 37

# Pray and walk in the Spirit

Lo, I have admonished you to *pray in the Spirit*, but do not forget that I have also commanded you to *WALK in the Spirit*, and this I expect not part of the time, but all the time.

The need is critical, the hour is late, and I am calling for full commitment from My own. You have desired to be chosen. Having been chosen, I would have you understand that I expect far more of you than of those who are not.

Romans 8:14-21

# Rely on My faithfulness

Do not be anxious. My Spirit shall direct your steps. You need have no fear. There is never a place where you walk that I have not preceded you. There are many times when your faith wavers. Take no account of it. I am keeping you even when you do not feel strong. You must rely on My faithfulness — not on your feelings.

Your strength will vary from day to day, but My power is always available to you as you yield to the Holy Spirit.

I Peter 1:3-9

# Only by a Person

I will bless you, My people, when your hearts turn to Me in earnestness and sincerity. From where shall your help come, except from the Lord? You search in vain for satisfaction from your worldly possessions.

Your soul can be nourished only by a *person* — not by any *thing;* and the only person adequate to meet the hunger of your soul is the Person of the Lord Jesus Christ, through the ministry of the blessed Holy Spirit.

John 6:51-58

# The central object

You shall hunger forever if you do not learn to feed on Christ. Your thirst shall never be quenched except you drink of the Spirit and partake of the Christ life. No mortal shall bless you thus.

The heart shall rejoice when Christ is the central and highest object of its affection. Dedication brings pure rapture when the desire is wholly fixed upon Him — Jesus! His Name alone, when breathed in adoration, lifts the weariest heart from despair and fills the seeking soul with exhilaration.

John 4:13, 14

## Let Him take the initiative

Let no selfish motives rule your actions. Be motivated by the love of God, and if you truly are, you can rest assured that whatever you do has the approval of your Father.

You cannot do with joy some of the things that may be permissible for another. You are not free to make your own choices as long as you are surrendered to the Will of God, for when you are yielded to Him, it is *He* who gives the directions. Wait for Him to take the initiative.

James 4:6-10

## Not lethargy but surrender

You are called not to lethargy but surrender.

Happy is the man who puts his trust in the Lord, yes, even to the extent that he lets Him formulate the plans and direct the goings.

No reward is sweeter than to feel His commendation. No life is more tranquil than that lived in His will. At His feet there is peace. Turmoil shall not dwell in the home where Christ is the honored guest.

All of life becomes a hymn of praise when God's love rules the heart.

I John 2:17

# Communication

Keep in vital communication with Me. Loose yourself from the world at every possible point. You can fulfill My purpose only when your channel is completely open and free to Me. Resist every hindrance. Yield to Me the deepest place in your consciousness. Only in this way do I have full control of your life energies. Otherwise you dissipate them in ignorance, unintentionally. I will preserve them for the Spirit's activity as you abide in the place of communion.

Do not look for any other secret of spiritual power. There is none.

Phil. 3:7-14

# Frugality and supply

You shall have My blessing as you bear the yoke, and in carrying My burdens there shall always be joy. I have called you for this ministry, and I will supply your needs so that you will not be weighed down with financial cares. Be willing to do without until I supply. Such as is needful I will give, and anything more would be a snare and a disappointment.

Luxuries burden the soul with guilt. Beauty I bless, but those vanities which only serve to feed pride are destructive to the soul. Learn to discern the difference between necessities and luxuries, and be content with modest things.

Leave off indulgences and follow the pattern of others who have learned this lesson. Let your soul be inspired by the character of those who are disciplined in frugality rather than permitting your eye to be attracted by the extravagance of someone else.

Prov. 15:16

# Take no thought for tomorrow

My children are never more well cared for than when they commit their earthly needs to Me and unceasingly give first place to My kingdom. I am not a pauper, neither will I let you be financially embarrassed; but I do forbid you to be concerned about these things. I need your attention centered on Me, and I cannot have that until you let go your earthly cares.

I do not forbid you to work; I only forbid you to WORRY. The best way to break the power of worry is to refuse to take thought for tomorrow. This is the key. Today is rarely a problem. Most anxious thoughts are related to the future. Put all of tomorrow into My keeping, and let your faith operate in this area.

For today you need Wisdom. For tomorrow you need Faith. Try it, and you will never want to go back to the old way.

Matt. 6:28-34

# The hour of visitation

Simplify your life. Labor not for that which perishes. Only the doing of the will of God is of any permanent value. You are dissipating your spiritual energies by too many activities. Over-involvement is a constant threat, even as it was to Jesus in His earthly ministry. Constantly he went alone to the mountain to pray in order to offset the daily pressure of the multitudes.

I have plans for you, and Mine preclude your own. I have work for you, and it shall come upon you swiftly and you will need to be free to undertake it. You shall not be bound if you make preparation now.

Know your hour of visitation.

Matt. 8:21, 22

# Responsibilities and privileges

Responsibilities always increase in proportion to privileges. He who is recipient of great spiritual riches, of him will I require much in the way of ministry. Let the earthly life of the Lord Jesus be an example to you. Day and night He toiled, praying by night and working by day. So must you. The present hour is even more critical because the time of final judgment is coming upon mankind. Darkness is deepening, and the light of My witness is more needed than ever before.

Be faithful, and you shall deliver others and preserve your own soul.

Matt. 25:28-30

# Fight procrastination

If you desire to share your faith with others, do not wait for a more convenient time. Life can only be lived in the present moment. Fight procrastination as an enemy; but before you can fight it, you need to be more alert as to its recognition, for it often masquerades in other more acceptable forms. Many times you do not allow Me to speak through you because you lack courage, but you deceive your own heart with the excuse that some future time and place will be more suitable.

When you are ready to act in implicit obedience to the Spirit, and thus remove the baffle of procrastination, you will then be confronted with your more basic weaknesses and I will help you with them.

Mark 8:35

# Exercise your faith

You are bound by pride and self-satisfaction. I am not pleased. I need your witness in a free flow. You must be more articulate. Exercise your faith, knowing that I will give you the right words and will fill them with the power of My Spirit, and they shall be used by Me to bring salvation and deliverance.

Be not detained by self-doubt. Rely on Me, and do not regard your own limitations as a liability.

I will manifest through you in a mighty way if you will only give Me the opportunity. Be My mouthpiece, and I will supply the words and the message.

Mark 16:20

# Anticipate surprises

O My daughter, be obedient. I have purposes for you. Lo, I say, *I* have purposes . . . *I* have a ministry for you. Look not to any man to open this door. I Myself open the doors to the places of service which I have in mind for My children. I not only open doors, but more often than otherwise, I CREATE the place of service, and, as it were, plant a new tree in virgin soil. I do not need in any way an already-existant plan . . . I make My own plans, and in order to reach the souls for whom I am concerned, I lead in new paths and down unpaved roads.

One Bible example of this is the account of Philip and his witness to the eunuch crossing the desert. (Acts 8:26) Another is the ministry that was opened by the woman of Samaria as she became suddenly a missionary to her own towns-people. (John 4:28, 29)

Be prepared for the unexpected, and anticipate surprises if you deign to follow Me.

To change the figure, keep your eye on the baton. I may introduce a sudden change not written in the score . . .a rest, a hold, a crescendo not indicated in the music.

# Vital contact

Live in constant communion with Me, and strive to maintain continual vital contact. So shall be generated within you the spiritual power which builds up a ready supply for the moments of actual ministry.

This is the reason Jesus spent long hours in lonely vigil with His Father. This is why the scriptures admonish you to pray without ceasing.

As you pray and meditate, you are enriched by the Spirit in the grace and compassion of Jesus Christ. Your soul is perfected as you kneel in His presence, even as a flower unfolds in the sunshine.

Jude 20, 21

# Boundless joy

Know in your heart that your vessel has been formed for the purpose of shedding abroad the glory of God, and the Spirit ministers in you to the end that this may be accomplished.

Lo, I stand at your side to help, and you shall never need to rely on your own strength or wisdom. As long as you bless and honor Me, the rivers of life shall flow forth and your joy shall be boundless.

II Cor. 4:7

# Be attentive

My child, as you listen, you shall hear My voice. I never speak to satisfy curiosity. You have need to know what is on My heart, and therefore I commune with you. Be attentive. Let your ear be always attuned to Me.

Nothing can shut Me out except indifference. Other people and outside forces cannot rob you of your communication with Me, but coldness in your own heart can dull your receptivity.

Be attentive to the Spirit of God. He will bless you richly. He will make you sensitive to divine guidance, even in mintue details, for what appears to be a small matter, very frequently is in reality of far-reaching consequences.

## Constant attention

Do not forfeit My nearness by preoccupation with any other joy. Know that the fullest measure of devotion to Me is not too much to give, and any less is sin. I need your constant attention. How else can I communicate with you without periodic interference? It is not too much to ask.

You shall be able to do all else that is demanded of you in the daily path of duty and not lose touch with Me in the Spirit if there is no division in your soul. All your life forces must be directed to Me.

Psalm 25:14, 15

## The oil of consecration

All your ministry must be blessed by the oil of consecration. Not one thing can be withheld. That which is most precious must be daily offered in dedication. Anything which is unworthy or evil must be given to Me so that it may be taken away; but the pure and good must be given to Me also, so that you may be continually freed from clasping it to yourself.

Anything you grasp becomes a burden. Give all to Me in a daily morning offering.

Leviticus 6:14-23

# Release the blessings also

You are accustomed to give Me liberty to take from you all that is displeasing to Me. Now I ask that you give Me daily all that blesses, yes, even the good which I bestow upon you. Give Me this also. I will bless it and protect it and safeguard it for you. Only in My care is it secure. Would you risk the dangers of holding it yourself?

All rest of heart comes through committal. You have been taught to release your burdens. Now I am endeavoring to help you relinquish your blessings. Part of your anxiety at this moment has come from a feeling of responsibility to the care of that priceless thing which I Myself have given you. So I say: Give it to Me! I will not TAKE it from you, but I will KEEP it for you, and thus it shall be twice blessed. You will be blessed in having received, and you will be freed from the burden of its protection. It is like placing a jewel in a vault. It is less accessible, but it is not GONE; only your concern for its safety it gone.

Let Me guard your treasure.

II Tim. 1:14


# As a lamb before a lion

All kinds of dangers lurk about you. The enemy would rob you of the most sacred blessing. He has no desire to take it except to destroy it. Your power to protect it is no match for his treachery. He lies in wait in the unexpected place, and you are as a lamb before a lion.

At My feet leave all, and know it is for your ultimate joy. Truly it is NOT a sacrifice. It will be your salvation.

I Peter 5:8

# The harvest is overripe

The hour is late. Be diligent. The harvest is overripe, and because it is so, there is need for greater care in the gathering of it. Do not be presumptuous. Do not rely on the same kind of methods you used in the past. There is need for greater tenderness. There is need for greater compassion. There is need for infinite patience. This is a delicate work. When you deal with the souls of men, you are touching the most precious thing there is. No work is more demanding of wisdom. Seek Me continually for direction and for understanding, so that you may be able to gather the overripe fruit without bruising it.

Joel 3:13

# The headship of Christ

Many are looking to you for deliverance and for salvation. Be aware of every possible moment of opportunity. The destiny, yes, the ETERNAL destiny of lives is at stake. A frivolous spirit or a careless indulgence in levity may rob both yourself and the other person of a priceless experience in the creative power of the Spirit of God. Don't take such a precarious path. Stay in the Spirit, and keep your mind in captivity to the mind and the thoughts of Christ. Be satisfied with nothing less. Anything less will cause you to be virtually unproductive.

I Pet. 1:12-19

# Discover the spiritual significance

Look to Me in the midst of every storm. Much shall be revealed. Life is charged with meaning whenever you discover the true spiritual significance of that which befalls you. Do not labor to understand, but simply yield each situation up to Me and worship Me in the center of it.

Illumination comes when the heart is submissive; but if you rebel and strike out at the unpleasant action, you will multiply your own distress and bring upon yourself destructive forces.

Psalm 37:1-19

## Faith manifesting in divine response

No evil can hurt you if you yield it up to Me, because simultaneously, as you do so, I bring to bear upon it forces of good. One example in the Bible is the visitation of angels for the preservation of Daniel as he was cast into the den of lions. It was the power of righteousness at work within the heart of Daniel that brought to his aid the protecting forces. It was faith and committal manifesting into divine response.

The same law will work for you. Test it and prove it. As you experience it in operation, you will find that your fear of calamity will gradually be dissolved, and you will gain a firmer inner confidence.

Daniel 6:22

## Faith and the delivering angel

"I slew the lion and the bear", said David, and having thus developed courage, he moves unflinchingly to confront the giant Philistine. That which had been tried in solitude broke into evidence in the public crisis. It was in this area of faith and courage that he was above his fellows.

Secret faith had its moment of open revelation. It is ever so. Build inner faith from the lesser challenges, and it will be your delivering angel in the most calamitous moment.

I Sam. 17:32-37

# A spirit of gratitude

O My little one, the path has been prepared before you, and you shall not fear, neither hesitate. As you tread, you will find the victory has already been won and the foe already defeated. No challenge shall turn you aside, and no past defeat shall dim your faith in My provision for today and My grace and strength for tomorrow.

Love Me with your whole heart. The blessing of the Lord rests upon all who dedicate their energies to devotion. I am the Lord, your God. I have saved you and healed you, and you have much for which to praise Me. Never stop. The highest occupation of the soul is that of worship and adoration. Never cease to keep a spirit of overflowing gratitude. It shall both sweeten your own spirit and lift your whole ministry into the highest plane.

Joshua 1:3-9

# Learn well and listen closely

No disturbance, either in yourself or in others, can interfere with the moving of My Spirit if you do not focus attention upon it.

Be as a babe in its mother's arms and know that I carry you near to My heart, and this is why you have knowledge of many things not revealed to others. They must find this place for themselves before they can hear My voice. Meanwhile, you are My ambassador to them.

Learn well, and listen closely.

Isaiah 26:3

# Put off the self life

Be aware of My presence. Your receptivity is dulled by undue involvement in unimportant pastimes. I need your full attention, yes, I need complete dedication.

These are the closing hours of this dispensation, and I am calling all My chosen to put off the self life and to walk in the Spirit. This is not a new message. It was the message of the apostles; indeed, it was the message of Jesus. It was also the message of the Psalms and Proverbs, insofar as they emphasize uncompromising loyalty to the truth, and outward actions that are consistent with inward convictions.

John 13:17

# Inner strength and outer action

Integrity and devotion have always been indispensable virtues. I say to you that in this hour of apathy and decline when the very foundations of mankind's moral structures are crumbling, you need to be more diligent than ever to find and to keep your own personal inner strength and to allow it to manifest in outer action.

Prov. 28:13

# Inner balance

By continual wearing away, the wheel becomes mis-shapen; so by constant aggravation of outward circumstances, your soul may lose its true form. Only as you keep the inner balance of your spirit true can you prevent distortion in the outward manifestation.

The outward is that which man sees, but the inward is the more vital. "Man looketh on the outward appearance, but God looketh upon the heart", and it is in the heart that integrity must be maintained at any price. No earthly joy is of any significant value by comparison. Never barter the one for the other. Never forfeit the inner peace for the outer joy. You are exchanging pearls for sand.

Psalm 51:6-17

# The centrifugal power of the Holy Spirit

All kinds of contrivances will seek to throw you off balance. The centrifugal power of the Holy Spirit within you is ever seeking to draw you and keep you in the perfect divine pattern and form. Do not resist it. Rather, resist the pull of the external forces. In the language of the scriptures, it is the world, the flesh and the devil which influence toward destruction and ugliness.

It is only the divine Spirit of God — nothing else — that can preserve your soul and life in the beauty of purity and the expression of grace.

Galatians 5:16-25

# The Spirit knows no decline

Seek Him in communion and in prayer. Seek Him without reservation. Seek Him, as it were, with the vigor of youth; for your spirit knows no decline with years — indeed, quite the opposite, for it increases in strength as it develops in understanding and gains experience.

The Lord is the strength of your life, and He knows no decline. His strength is eternal: it never increases nor decreases. It has never been less and shall never be more.

Psalm 27:1

# A garment of glory

My holy life surrounds you like a globe of light. It is not visible to the natural eye, but it is witnessed by angels and they rejoice. Yes, and it is visible to the devil, and he knows that he is powerless to touch you.

You are in this place of divine protection by your own choice. You were not aware that this is what you were choosing, but at every point where you desire My holiness and My will above your own, you fashion a garment of glory for the soul. You may feel encouraged in knowing that you have it now, but lo, I say unto you, there is a day coming, and that very soon, when the protection of My presence in light around you shall deliver your very soul out of destruction.

Intrigue shall not lay hold upon you, and man shall not bring to pass any influence strong enough that you cannot resist as long as you put your trust in Me.

Psalm 91:9, 10

# Sincerity

O My child, be truly as a little child, and preserve within your spirit the grace of simplicity. Maintain a candid honesty. Resist all temptation to put on airs. Be natural. Strive to be as Jesus, who was never pretentious, never evasive nor coy. Be real, be sincere, for to serve God demands sincerity. The needs of hearts and problems of life are real. Many carry burdens and griefs, and how can you be of help in a frivolous state of mind?

I Peter 5:8

# Guard against foolishness

Joy is a medicine to the grieving heart and broken spirit. You may have My joy in abundance, but guard your own spirit against foolishness. Thoughts of nonsense and empty words are utter waste. I can use them in no way at all. They are a detriment and never an attribute.

All words are either actively good or actively negative, and if they are negative, they are worse than empty, they are destructive. They will act to nullify the testimony I would establish when you speak My words, so that if you mix the two, the good will be cancelled out by the evil.

You cannot afford such carelessness. My servants must be wise as serpents and blameless as doves. Let your EVERY word be full of grace and taste of the saltiness of divine goodness. Let it be known of you by your good conversation that you have been much with Me, and be on your guard lest the enemy sow the tares of careless words which will spring up and choke the precious grain of divine truth.

Matthew 12:36, 37

# Words of healing

Speak evil of no man, but conceal the evil by speaking that which is good. (Love covers a multitude of sins, and it is the glory of love to conceal a matter.) In so doing you will heal, not wound. You desire to have a healing ministry. Let it embrace both the body and the soul, and be not content to heal bodies while wounding souls.

Learn to minister blessing and comfort to the spirit through your words and thus enhance the ministry of physical healing.

Colossians 4:6, 3:16

# You are violating My will

My child, you are not where I would have you be. How can I be pleased with you? "Love", it is written, "seeketh not her own". But you have been pursuing your own ends, and this to Me is folly. What you desire may be beautiful and good, and may constitute nothing that is harmful in itself: all the same, you are violating My will and marring My pattern.

Romans 15:1-3


# The King's business

I require of you a dedication of purpose that can tolerate no deflection from the prescribed path of action. Be not beguiled by the world, neither by your best intentions. You are not on a pleasure trip, but on the mission of an ambassador. There is no room for casual banter and fleshly exaltation in the King's business.

Heb. 12:1


# A way-preparer

Be tolerant of all, at whatever stage of spiritual development they may be, but do not set your standards by theirs. I am moving, and I want you to be a way-preparer. Get into the front ranks, and hold your position. Never flinch. Certainly I can expect you never to turn coward and flee!

Give Me the privilege of sustaining you in the dangerous position. Think you not that I am well able to keep you there and adequately supply every needed grace?

I Cor. 16:13

# As My magnet

Many there are whom I am drawing, and what will you if I have chosen to use you as My magnet? A magnet's effectiveness is constituted by virtue of what it IS. It cannot of itself either move nor speak. It simply IS, and on the strength of what it is, it exerts its influence. One thing only is necessary for its operation — that is to be brought into proximity and working distance to the other object. Even so, let Me move you by My hand into the places of vital influence.

All the rest of the work I will accomplish through the power of My Spirit within you.

# Dismiss with dispatch

Nothing I am doing would seem strange to you if you had been more attentive to My voice. No fog of doubt would obscure My face if you were in the place of My direction.

I can lead you only as you wait upon Me for guidance. Man will always take you down the wrong path. You should have learned this lesson well by this time. It is folly to stumble along in blindness. I am your FRIEND. Can you not trust My love? Would I ever harm you? Do I not give you a full measure of joy? Give freely to others, regardless of their actions, and never look upon any circumstance as untoward.

NOTHING can bring you unhappiness unless you put yourself in its path. Let it pass by, nor countenance even the passing. Give it not the dignity of recognition. All that you discount shall be as vapor. It can achieve no substance. It shall be a passing mist.

Jesus never grappled with a demon: He dismissed them with dispatch and finality, and often indicated more concern for the loved ones of the possessed than for the victim himself. You will find in this the guidance you need.

Mark 5:18-20

# Resist anxiety

The path that leads to victory is not straight and easy: it winds amid the vicissitudes of life. It is sometimes almost lost amid the perplexities of circumstances. It is not always in the light, but there are stretches that wind on through almost total darkness. In these places in particular you need to keep your hand in Mine. The darkness is no problem to Me. My heart rejoices in these places as I see your faith being strengthened and your courage high.

Press on, nor reach out to anything along the way for support. I Myself will uphold you and will keep you from stumbling. I will not allow you to lose your way nor step off the path. Where the road is rough and steep, I will give you special attention and care.

Remember the word of scripture that says "He goeth before". Surely, I DO go before, and I know aforetime all that you will encounter. Before you come to it, I know what lies ahead.

Resist the temptation to anxiety. Lean upon My promises. Even in the dark I can see the rainbow above your head. Remember, there would have been no bow had there been no storm.

# Worry closes My hand

Praise Me continually: so shall you bring joy to My heart, and in My rejoicing I will give you more than you need. Scripture commands you to give cheerfully, or hilariously. I will give to you likewise. Worry closes My hand. I cannot respond to worry; I can only wait until you cease worrying and begin praising.

Lift the song of praise without any shadow of dismay, and you will open to yourself and your family the floodgates of glory.

You shall become a witness to Me of the victory I can give which only the yielded can receive. Thus shall others be challenged to learn this secret also.

# The dynamic of miracles

O My child, lie quietly in My hand. The dynamic of miracles is here. Your own weakness is of no consequence, for I would vest you with My power. Your insignificance shall be swallowed up in My Presence.

My Presence is all about you, even all through you. Unless you resist Me, you cannot fail, for I cannot fail and you are in Me, kept by the power of God. Strengthen your heart with this truth.

Acts 1:8

# Discover the power of Truth

Discover the power of Truth — any truth. Put it to the test. Every truth is as firm as God Himself. It can be relied upon. It can be trusted as a fact and counted upon in experience.

Believe My truths, but go beyond this. Put them into operation, and learn what it is to experience them as well. Only in this way can you proclaim their fact in a persuasive manner. No teaching is effective except as it springs out of experience, and no teaching which does spring from experience shall fall short.

Teaching will be easy and spontaneous and forceful whenever it is the overflow of life. You cannot teach about Me any other way, because I am not a cold fact, but a Living Person. So My Truth is *living truth*. It shall split the rocks of doubt and break forth in the most unlikely places.

Drop the seeds of Truth. I will accomplish My purpose.

Heb. 4:12

# Do not presume upon My patience

My children, the hour is late. Call not upon Me for help after you have hopelessly lost your way, but seek Me now for guidance so clear that you will never be led astray.

The mercy of God is great toward the lost and the backslider, but I say unto you, this is no day to live idly nor walk in any careless fashion.

Do not depend upon My patience and presume upon My tolerance. You despise My laws, and pray for healing. You starve your soul of the nourishment of My Word, and pray for grace. You neglect prayer, and yet expect to be conscious of My nearness.

I say unto you: seek out the holy place of communion, and you shall have restored unto you the joy of your salvation. Feed your soul and your mind upon My Word, and you shall be strengthened and enriched.

Keep My commandment, walk circumspectly, and don't even glance in the direction of compromise.

Psalm 19:13

# Spiritual dependency

The life which you draw from God is like the sap in the tree which must be drawn from the bosom of the earth. Sever the roots from the source, and death ensues. Even so, the spiritual dependency of your soul upon Him, though unseen, is every bit as real.

Draw upon Him. It is His desire to sustain you. It is His will and His design. It is your only hope, your only comfort.

*It is PRAYER!*

Psalm 1:3

# Inner communion

Bow before Me in adoration and humility and you need not stoop before any man. Give Me your hand to hold and you need not the support of a single human being. Know that when I place upon your ministry the seal of Mine approval it shall no longer be important to you whether or not you are accepted by any other.

This is an activity in which we are co-laborers together — I and you and the Father. Keep a strong awareness of this identification. You will lose the anointing if you allow anyone to enter and distract.

Stay in the holy place of inner communion and I will break forth through your vessel and manifest My glory outwardly.

Mark 6:11-13

# An anointed tongue

I have called you to a special ministry, and it cannot be carried out properly without My full blessing.

Let Me anoint your tongue, and you shall speak with divine authority and never again will you say, "I am a weak and inadequate vessel". I shall put words into your heart and speak them forth from your lips, and hearts shall burn as the message goes out.

You shall know that it is My message and My words that are spoken. The fruits you shall offer up to Me, for you shall know truly that it is the Lord your God who has brought to pass His own word of promise.

Luke 10:1-16

# Requirements of discipleship

Come unto Me, and I will give you rest. My way is so easy. You need only take My hand and let Me guide you — simply listen to My voice and let Me instruct you. When you were a little child, you did your mother's bidding. It was not an arduous task but a life of simplicity motivated by the mutual interests of the family. So it is in My household. Each ministers to the other, and all unto Me. It is a beautiful and natural mingling together of common concerns and expressions of love in service that is for the most part almost unconsciously expressed in the ordinary routine of the day.

It is a subtle deception of the carnal mind that pushes the requirements of discipleship up beyond the reach of the shortest member of God's family. You can more readily reconcile your failures if you can persuade yourself that My commandments are unattainable to you at your present level of development. I am not less considerate than a mother, but fit the task assigned to the age and ability of each of My children. Obedience, to Me, is achievement, whether it is the five-year-old who sets the table or the fifteen-year-old who bakes a cake.

Let Me teach you how to work in My kingdom. Surely I will fit the task to your capabilities. There is a path of obedience in which you may walk today, a task for which you are prepared, a duty which you may perform for Me without fear of failure. I am not unreasonable.

# Counsel with Me

Be not disturbed by evildoers. They are in My hand to do as I please, even as are the righteous. I have certain things to accomplish which could not be brought to pass without this avenue of operation. Do not be alarmed. All is under My control. Stand upon My Word, and let your only support be your faith in Me. I Myself will hold you up and keep you from swaying.

What goes on in the lives of others need not distress you. I will deal with them, and indeed, can do so effectively only as they turn to Me alone. Your well-intended 'help' is not needed, but may be a decided detriment. They are on an entirely different path from you, and you cannot join them without forsaking My will and My best for you. Live in Me. Walk in Me. Counsel with Me, and look to Me alone for your direction and your encouragement.

I will minister to you as you wait upon Me, and I know precisely what help you need, even as a physician selects the proper prescription for his patient. I will similarly give you what you need for health of soul and strength of spirit.

Go your way in peace and in rejoicing. The Lord your God is with you and will be your helper.

Romans 11:8; Isaiah 6:10

## The course lies dead ahead

The time will come that you will say, *"Surely the Lord was in this place and I knew it not"*. For I say to you, My Spirit broods upon the waters, even upon the waters of difficulty, and I shall bring out of the chaotic condition in your life a trophy and a witness of My grace. For, as the Bible says, *"Where sin abounded grace did much more abound."* Be not dismayed, neither be turned aside. Set your heart with even greater diligence to follow the Spirit. Others may find Me and lose Me again. Be not discouraged because of this. What navigator would set his course by the location of other ships? You have a harbor to make, and you have a course to follow and that course lies dead ahead.

Storm nor wind shall not detain you. These things are without substance in the mind of the Spirit. The enemy would tell you that they have substance. The Spirit will wipe them away as a thin mist if you will determine to walk on in faith. You will look back and see no trace of them and marvel that you faltered.

I Cor. 15:57, 58

# Be not afraid of solitude

I have a ministry for you. You have not found it yet because you have been earnestly and in sincerity and with humble heart trying to conform to the patterns of others.

Be not afraid of solitude. You will not lose My touch. You will not miss a blessing. How shall the hand of any other bring you greater joy or clearer insight than I can bring to you Myself? Do you recall the words of scripture, *"you need not that any man teach you because the anointing dwelleth in you"?* One life blesses another life, and you learn some by observation and fellowship, to be sure; but all of this pales like the faltering flame of a match in the blinding rays of the sun when compared to the fuller light and the deeper fellowship that can and must be found in extended vigils alone with Me.

I John 2:27


# Perspective and depth

You need perspective and depth. This never comes from public converse, but from private communion. You seek to learn from others, but I long to tell you things I may never be able to tell them. I say this not to tempt you to feel proud, but to explain to you that I do not share the same truths with all. There are truths I wish to give YOU. You may never be asked to share them with any other person. They may be just for you — or they may be for people you have never seen as yet.

Mark 9:2-9

# Prepare your garments

The day is at hand, and the Day Star riseth even now. You may not see Him yet, but He is only just beneath the rim of the horizon, and you shall behold Him shortly in all His glory.

How ought you to rise and make yourself ready! How you should put your house in order and prepare your garments!

Your garments shall be of fine linen, for it is the righteousness of the saints.

Rev. 19:8

# Ionospheric Christian living

Stay in the flexibility of the Spirit. Live in the faith realm, and let your thoughts soar freely in the open skies of faith, where the things not yet seen become real to you. Call it ionospheric Christian living, if you wish. It will free you from bondages to people. It will not give you an independent nor rebellious feeling toward others, but will liberate you so that you will no longer feel the need to struggle against these hindrances.

I will lift you out of the bondage as I brought the body of Jesus out of the graveclothes. How I wish I could bring all My people into this kind of liberty. Indeed, if I can only find individuals in whom I can bring this to pass, perhaps through their witness, the worshiping groups may catch the vision. Indeed, if you yourself can find it, you may be able to lead your own group into it and thus open a new path for them!

Gal. 5:1

# The golden path

O My daughter, I have a special path for you. Search it out diligently. Let Me — let ME guide you in it. Follow not other sheep aimlessly as they roam through My pastures. Lo, I call you to follow ME. To change the figure, let ME be your instructor, your teacher. Follow not the pupils, nor copy from their work.

I have you on a path which is all your own — rather, it is Mine . . . it is My way for you. It is not My way for anybody else. You shall never find it by observation. It will become clear to you only by REVELATION. This can only come from ME.

I call it *the golden path.* It is the golden path for you. It is a sacred secret between us. Guard it and keep it, and treasure it in the secret places of your soul. I will make a new, deep place within you where I will do a work by My own hand, and bring forth a treasure of My own making.

Amos 3:7


# I do not send storms

*Dear Jesus, in the hollow of Thy hand there is peace.*

Yes, My child, but do not ask Me to give you peace when you have removed yourself from My hand or if you are unwilling to rest quietly there. I give My peace to all who love and serve Me with singleness of heart. Any duplicity either in character or in aim shall bring disquiet.

I do not *send* storms upon your soul. They are generated by the pressures of your disobedience.

My people shall not rest, saith the Lord, for their hands are full of iniquity, their souls are filled with violence, and their hearts with deceit. Only in repentance shall they find peace, and only in singleness of heart shall they find joy.

Isaiah 57:21

# Draw upon His life force

Draw upon the life force of the Eternal, and as you do, your strength will be increased. If you fail to draw, you shall be at the mercy of your own weakness.

God is the source. He is the stream of energy that flows into your own heart. Guard the connection and the communication. Know that your constancy in waiting upon Him is all-important. It is essential to your victory.

Romans 8:11

# A sacrificial portion

O My little one, take courage; let your heart be strong, for I am near. I am your strong support: I will not allow your foot to slip. I will give you security and comfort, and you will know that it is from My own hand that it has come.

Look not about for love to come to you; look rather to see where you may give it. Do not tarry for convenience nor opportunity. Give a sacrificial portion. Make the out-of-season gesture of kindness.

Let not another sun set upon your indifference. You have fallen into the snare of thoughts of self and personal security rather than of self-giving. You have sought to receive rather than to give. This I can never bless. I love you too much to make provision for the comfort of your flesh.

Give generously, and give heartily. Lay not your giving alongside anyone else's. If your capacity has been enlarged, then I expect that much more of you. You shall not over-expend yourself. You have been remiss and have become in similar measure impoverished. Make no excuses, and reckon not the cost.

Give unstintingly, both of yourself and of your means. I will provide abundantly to meet all your needs.

# Healing for grief

*Dearest Jesus, how can I speak to Thee of all my heart feels? Shall I gather up every sorrow and bring them all to Thee as in a basket? Shall I fill a vial with my tears and give it unto Thee? Lo, shall I not keep back my fears, lest it grieve Thy heart to find I have so many?*

Nay, My child, I have long since embraced both yourself and your every burden. I have known the depth of your sorrow even before you tasted of its bitterness. I have borne away the sting of all your grief and you need not be tormented by it any longer. As soon as you see that I have dealt already with your case, you shall be able immediately to take unto yourself the comfort I have for you and to be blessed by receiving the balm I offer you.

There is no stigma in grief. There is no condemnation on My part toward you because you have sorrow; but in My love, I long to take from your heart every feeling that if allowed to remain would become destructive of your peace and would inflict a wound upon your soul.

I would heal every painful thought, and I would give you My joy: yes, even My joy at a time such as this. My Kingdom is righteousness and peace and joy in the Holy Spirit. You may have it under any and every circumstance, and you shall experience it more and more fully as you become aware that it is there for you for the asking, and yes, simply for the *taking*. What is already provided needs not to be requested.

Take from Me largely. I will make your cup to overflow. I will comfort you with a comfort so sweet that you will search in vain for words to describe it.

*Blessed be the Lord, for He hath not left me desolate!*

Psalm 147:3

# The earth, Thy habitation

*Open Thou mine eyes, O Lord, to behold Thy greatness. Thy majesty is above the heavens: Thy gentleness is as tender as a delicate flower. Thou art simultaneously powerful and kind. Thou art at the same moment justice and grace. Thou thunderest from the heavens, and the earth quakes at the sound of Thy voice. Thou singest in the midst of the congregation, and Thy saints rejoice and their spirit is strengthened.*

*Let us know Thee, O God. Let us know Thee in Thy glory, and let us worship Thee in the full light of Thy holiness. Let Thy Name be made known to the nations. Let the earth become Thy habitation.*

Zeph. 3:17

# Judgment at the house of God

Lo, My people, this is the day of battle. You shall set your forces in array. Sound the trumpet in Zion — the battle cry in the holy mountain. I shall come to destroy evil, and what will ye if My sword be already dipped in blood?

Judgment, it is written, shall begin at the house of God. Ere I set about to purge the world of evil, I shall verily purge My church. I shall not tolerate corruption and wink at open transgression as you have so freely done. You have regarded holiness with contempt, and you have rewarded perverseness and trickery with honor.

You have promoted the profane man and preferred the carnal and the clever above the simple and the pure. You have not asked My counsel, nor will I force it upon you. You have ignored Me and closed your eyes. Judgment shall overtake you while you are unprepared and unable to guard yourself against it. Mercy shall fail, and you shall find your hand-hewn cisterns have broken and run dry. You shall thirst, and your thirst shall remain unquenched.

Because you have forsaken Me, the well of living water, lo, I have turned My back upon you, and you shall perish in your chosen wilderness way. Except you repent, you shall perish even with the wicked; for you know My truth, but you pulled away the shoulder, and deliberately chose the path of self-will. You have walked in the flesh instead of in the Spirit, and you have thus repudiated your confession of trust in Me. (I Pet. 4:17-19)

Jer. 2:13

# I have built a hedge

Praise Me in the sanctuary. Praise Me in the solitary place of communion and prayer. Lift your heart, yes, lift it in gratitude; for My goodness surpasses knowing, and My mercies are ofttimes concealed from your eyes. In your sleeping and your waking hours, My hand of protection and blessing is upon you. Many a calamity would have overtaken you were it not for My care.

I have built a hedge about you, even as was written concerning Job. This was not a false accusation of the devil to Job: it was an actual reality. I only removed it to test and to prove him, and to put to silence the enemy of his soul. But for multitudes of My children I have never removed the hedge. Many can testify, "The Lord has been on my right hand and on my left, and I have not been distressed". Likewise, I am keeping you, My child, and for one purpose in particular — that you be able to accomplish the task committed to you and carry out to completion your ministry in the Spirit. Therefore, give diligence to your mission, and do not allow ease nor sloth nor levity to rob your soul of its stamina.

Job 1:10

# Resist indolence

You could easily fill your days with frivolous or selfish pursuits. Guard your time and energies, as they are the material from which the spiritual ministries are of necessity channeled. Dissipate your physical strength, or carelessly waste your time, and thus shall the Spirit be thwarted. By wickedness a man may do violence and injury to himself or his fellow-man, but simple indolence is by itself a militant force against the Spirit. Resist it in the full recognition of the destructive power that it is.

Determine in your heart to respond immediately to every prompting of the Spirit. Never dispute, for He is always right, and there can be no ramifications.

Prov. 24:30, 31

# True peace and false

Peace is in the full expression of My will. Anything short of this is a false peace. There is a dullness of spirit . . . a sort of stupor that overtakes the one who is no longer spiritually sensitive. This is often mistaken for true peace in a way that can be compared to the freezing man who feels sleepy, not knowing he is slipping into the very jaws of death. *There is a way which seems right to a man,* said the writer of Proverbs, *but the end thereof are the ways of death.* (Prov. 14:12)

Let not this sort of thing befall you. Make sure that your peace is the result of actively being in the will of God, and permit yourself no indulgence in selfishness.

# Preparation

My child, I would speak to you as to a disciple. What is in your hand? Would you attempt to do a work with broken instrument? You desire to serve Me in many ways. Have you carefully prepared? Or do you expect Me to overrule your lack of wisdom? Lo, I say unto you, PREPARATION is your own responsibility. Certainly I will help you in it, but I am not glorified through a vessel that is careless concerning its condition.

II Tim. 2:15

# Restoration

You are the keeper of your own soul. You hold the power to effect its perfection in that your will is the deciding factor. It is, as it were, the drive shaft, and the Holy Spirit is the power source. The two must work together — My Spirit, and your will. If the will becomes impotent because of sin or disobedience, there must be RESTORATION before there can again be effective operation of the Spirit in your life.

Rom. 6:11-16

# Motivation

Confession, repentance, and prayer strengthen the will to move in the direction of holiness. No one is brought into a life of holiness by outside force. The inner desire is always the first and the foremost motivation. As soon as the desire for righteousness is present, the Holy Spirit will immediately fill it with His own energy and bring the soul into victory.

II Chron. 7-14

# Look for the good

In the press of life I am your constant source of strength. When you pass safely through a difficult trial, you may know with certainty that it is I who have brought you through the test.

True knowledge is never acquired except by experience. Information may be gathered in abundance, but any deep knowing within the soul comes only as I teach you in the midst of real life experiences.

Much of the stress of life would be removed if you had more faith in the fact that I truly reign as absolute sovereign over EVERY situation in which you find yourself. Lo, I say to you, it is by divine appointment. Look always for the good which I am bringing out of it, and refuse to let the enemy disturb you with doubts.

Rejoice. Victory will be more complete and will come more quickly. I stand watching, and I will not let you fail.

Rom. 8:28

# Balm of Gilead

My child, whatever befalls, know it is from My hand. In the midst of every circumstance, I am your strength. In every heartache, I am your comfort. In every trial, I am your courage. Nothing can enter your life that I cannot transform into a blessing. No man can take anything from you that I cannot restore an hundredfold.

Let your heart be at rest. You may enjoy a deep, settled peace that no disturbance can destroy. It is maintained by your confidence in My love.

Place in My care both yourself and all you hold dear. Let the balm of Gilead restore your soul, and let joy be your portion. I will uphold you and you shall look to none else.

Release all anxiety. I am watching over you.

Isa. 26:3

# Salvation

*Work out your own salvation,* says the scripture, *for it is GOD who worketh in you both to will and to do of His good pleasure.* Thus, when you are conscious of spiritual weakness, do not wait for Me to move upon you to effect a change from without, but assume the responsibility for your weakened condition as though you were indeed your own saviour. In the self-same moment, My grace will do the rest!

Wholeness is the product of the Spirit, but it cannot come until your own desire sets it in motion.

Phil. 2:12, 13

# A burning torch

In every place where one of My faithful children stand, it is as a burning torch. The eyes of angels behold the light and rejoice that at these points darkness is arrested. If each child of God were aware of the blessing dispensed to those within his radius of influence, he would guard his light with utmost concern.

Carelessness is a temptation only when personal responsibility is overlooked. Nothing is more devastating to the ongoing of My kingdom than burned-out torches.

# Gentleness

Be obedient to My commands: so shall I bless you. Let Me guide you: thus shall you know the right path. Follow always the call of the Spirit. All who listen shall hear. Move with the flexibility of a yielded will. Mercies are laid up in store for the humble.

Gentleness of spirit brings overcoming power. It is not the strong will, but the YIELDED will that is blessed in My sight.

Mic. 6:8

# Grace

Follow righteousness, and pursue it with unmitigated fervor. It is the *only* pursuit that is legitimate for the Christian. I have given My promise that I will supply every other need if you seek righteousness. It is in the selfless abandon to the Spirit that grace is nurtured.

I have freely extended My grace *to* you. Now I desire to see My grace developed *in* you!

Hoseah 6:3

# Release others

No power on earth can thwart My purposes. I move through the center of every obstacle. I do not need to REMOVE the difficulty. It is no real problem to Me. It is only an anxiety manifesting itself in your mind and claiming the power to destroy. Indeed, it shall exert a destructive action if you fail to identify it and deal with it in proper fashion.

I am restricted when you hold negative thoughts about the actions of other people. Release them to Me; otherwise you turn the action upon yourself to your own hurt.

Be as a child in My care. Take no thought of second causes.

Gen. 50:20; Rom. 12:14

# Unquestioning trust

Let Me bless you. You need My blessing more than you need the help of all others combined. How often have I asked you to FOLLOW Me? I look to see you following, and instead I see you standing still and reckoning — or worse, fainting by the wayside.

It is your TOTAL commitment for which I wait. It is your unquestioning trust for which I yearn. It is your love flowing in utter simplicity which alone opens your channel to receive My mercies.

You can turn your burdens into blessings by giving Me EVERYTHING.

Prov. 3:5


# Patience and perfection

Patience, My child, is not a matter of forethought nor self control. Patience is the child of Tolerance. It will manifest itself quite naturally and without effort when the soul is rid of all resentment against imperfection. Perfection is the goal toward which a man strives, but perfection is never attained as long as man is in his mortal body. Purity of heart is possible, in a measure, but perfection is a word that could have been used to describe only a few rare souls, and then only relatively.

It is often your intolerance for your own and other's imperfections which gives rise to feelings of frustration and impatience. The only way you can make any reasonable progress toward perfection is by committing your entire life into My hands and realizing it is I who live within you and effect whatever changes are made. When you understand this, it will be easy for you to accept all shortcomings with the confidence in your heart that as you look constantly to Me, I work within you to bring to pass My purposes, and I fashion you into a vessel of beauty and usefulness.

Ask of Me, and perhaps I will show you the pattern by which I am shaping your life, and you will come to know that My grace, My strength, My love are great enough to bring the work to its conclusion.

James 1:2-4

# Tensions build fortitude

Many perplexities bring you closer to Me, for as you seek wisdom and need courage, you are driven to Me for help. I purposely remove the support of friends in order that you will look to Me alone. These are the times you become pliable in My hands. Self-will thrives on success, and the sins of the disposition are rarely exposed in gaiety. It is the moments of crisis that reveal either a man's strength or his weakness. It is the tensions of life that build fortitude or expose fear.

I am in your midst to remove your anxieties, to show you your inadequacies, and to teach you how to draw from Me all the fortitude you need in any situation. Know that I keep you, that I love you, that I fully understand. Cast yourself wholly upon My mercy. Pray, knowing that the request is already granted and the help already provided.

Act in faith: it is the secret of every victory.

James 1:12


# Trials

Many trials beset the righteous, but surely I am your deliverer. In a multitude of storms and adversities I temper the spirit. I mold and shape through circumstances: I bend and fashion through grief and pain. Out of all these things I cause the patient soul to rise to a place of clearer vision and deeper understanding.

Rom. 12:12

# Thorns in the nest

In every situation, I control the forces that bear upon your life. Do not question circumstances. Look to Me for an understanding of your inner responses. The outer you can seldom alter. It is as you receive insight as to your own feelings that a work of grace is accomplished in your soul.

Remember always that it is in the spiritual realm that I am working. Man looks upon the natural, physical world: My concern is for your spiritual life, that virtues may develop in you. While you are praying for a problem to be solved, a need to be met, a thorn to be removed from your nest, I am watching to see if any divine virtue will manifest in your responses to pressure. I am looking for true faith to express in the time of want, and I am waiting to see when the thorns in the nest will cause you to move out and try your unused wings.

II Cor. 4:17, 18

# Complaint is devastating

I allow no adversity to come without a hidden purpose . . . hidden to you, but waiting to be revealed as you seek spiritual understanding.

The reason why complaint is so devastating to the soul is because the moans of despair drown the voice of God that would bring insight.

You cannot listen to Me while you are voicing complaints. State the case; commit it to ME, and I will give you MY solution.

Prov. 17:22

# Guard your thoughts

Guard the thoughts of your soul and test them by the love of Jesus. Let no intention become an action until it has passed this test. In this way, many failures and much regret can be avoided.

Live in freedom and in peace, for angels watch over you, and My Spirit dwells within. Count upon My help. My love enfolds you. My love never fails. Let it possess you, and all shall be well.

You are in the midst of much that is challenging and bewildering, but be convinced of this one thing: I have placed you here. My purpose shall unfold.

Romans 8:28

# The attribute of mercy

Mercy is one of My attributes which I strongly desire you to have. Mercy is become so uncommon in human actions that even the word itself is seldom heard or used.

If you are not merciful, it would have been better had you not presumed to become My disciple. Without this quality in ministry, there can be no genuine blessing flowing through your life. In each relationship with others, if you do not have mercy, you will blight, not bless.

Without mercy, Calvary would have become a preachment of condemnation rather than of forgiveness. Expressing, as He did, His mercy toward His enemies, He provided you an example of the extent to which your own compassion should operate. You may never achieve an expression of love in the same degree, but let it be always the measure and the guide by which you judge your own attitudes.

Matt. 5:7

# Look for Me in the fiery furnace

In a multitude of circumstances the soul is tested, and often you may experience many different pressures bearing in upon you all at the same time. This in itself works toward a special grace, for it demands greater stamina than any one challenge met singly, however difficult that one might be.

Cold, hunger, peril, separation, if they came upon you at one time, as could very well be the case, how would you respond? Modern man has so protected himself from discomfort and from unpleasantness that both his body and his soul are in a dangerously weakened condition. Where shall he draw courage in the day of affliction? How shall he face privation and worldly loss? What then shall his life testify of his confidence and joy in God? (Phil. 4:12) Let him know that I try him now in lesser degrees to prepare him to pass triumphantly through what is ahead.

Never try to smooth out the way for either yourself or another who is passing through a trial unless you have been definitely led to do so. Your intentions may be noble, but your actions may prove a disfavor from My vantage point, because you may by your kindness thwart My work in that vessel.

*Always* you need My guidance, even for your acts of benevolence. It is almost as hard to watch another suffer as to do so yourself, but you would find it easier if you could see My divine hand at work.

Look for Me in the midst of every fiery furnace and you will be influenced by My Spirit in your actions and reactions rather than by your own natural impulses. (II Cor. 11:16-32 II Tim. 2:3)

Daniel 3:25

# The larger life

Never let your inadequacies be a handicap. Give them to Me, and they will become My opportunity to demonstrate My power operating through you in response to your plea for aid. I would never have a chance to help you if you were always self-sufficient and capable of meeting every challenge. It is at those points where you are obviously lacking that you can discover that greater forces are at work for you beyond your own abilities and knowledge.

Be ready to move in faith every time you sense inadequacy, and in each experience, as you trust Me, you will experience what is meant by "the larger life", and I will fill all your lack with My divine undertaking, for I will surely undertake for you and bring you out with a testimony unto My Name.

II Cor. 12:9, 10

# A crucial hour

Watch for the signs of My soon-coming. Do not be blind to that which is transpiring around you and in the world. It has been revealed to you what you may expect. No concern lies more heavily on My heart than the preparation of My chosen ones for the ingathering. Man cannot anticipate the turn of fate in his own life, so events come upon him and overtake him unaware. I do not want My coming to be so and catch you by surprise. Not only do you need to prepare your own hearts, but I would use you to warn and help others.

This is no time for apathy. There has been no more crucial hour in all man's history.

Luke 21:34-36

# Simplicity of spirit

By simplicity of spirit the soul is protected against forces of destruction. He who clings to My hand in childlike trust shall walk with joy in a path of safety. His utter confidence in Me is a safeguard against that which otherwise would come against him from the reasonings of his own mind. He who seeks to preserve his own soul by the devices of his own intellect will be snared and brought into confusion and bondage.

The soul progresses by praise, worship and love, but it is hindered by conscious thought and effort. This may seem strange, but it can easily be proven by experiment. Jesus taught this in his reference to the lilies of the field, how they neither toil nor spin, but are clothed by the Father. Even so, said He, a man does not add to his physical stature by conscious effort. I say to you, what is true in the natural is true in the spiritual.

Lay at My feet the anxiety about your own spiritual life, and give yourself to love Me and to worship Me. The results in your soul will be joy and victory. You shall know that I am your total sufficiency, and that truly My grace is sufficient and My strength within sustains you, and your own weakness shall not be a handicap, for I am greater.

Luke 18:17


# Never initiate

My child, go not without My direct guidance. Never be moved by outside influences alone. Check every action. Know that any move you make that is not confirmed in the Spirit is bound to bring confusion to all concerned. Be certain it is MY will, and be not influenced by man.

For every move that I initiate, I clear the way and there is no strain or confusion.

Psalm 32:8

# The art of constancy

Let nothing draw your attention away from Me. In the midst of every legitimate activity your soul can be focused on Me if gratitude and adoration and worship have captured your heart. The intellect can be occupied with all manner of other things, but the soul of a man may be a continual chapel of praise as you learn the art of constancy in loving Me first and foremost.

The first commandment is that you love the Lord your God with all your heart, soul, mind and strength. (Mk. 12:30) You frequently emphasize how MUCH you should love Me. This is important, but even more important to Me, *and to you*, is the constancy of your love . . . that it be the overflowing grace of your heart *continually*, so that every waking hour you are truly and literally walking and worshiping in the Spirit.

Anything less is a disappointment to Me and will make you correspondingly weaker in your personal life and witness.

Heb. 13:15

# I await your desire

O My child, truly I rejoice in ministering to an open heart. I have so much to give and so few truly desire to receive. My soul is enlarged with grieving because My people are so callous of spirit and so hard of heart. I would give so much more abundantly if they would but ask.

I await your desire, because if I gave to you when your desire was small, you would not be prepared for receiving.

Hide nothing from Me. Bring Me everything, and repent of anything you cannot offer Me as a holy gift. I would sanctify your entire life. Anything with which I cannot deal because of your resistance shall be a hindrance to you, and shall bring you only sorrow. Release all to Me.

Luke 18:22-24

# Harmony of purpose

If My people honor Me in their hearts, I will put My word upon their lips. Those who seek to live in obedience to My commandments will be brought into conformity with My nature, and these will I use to fulfill My purposes. Do not men do likewise? When a man chooses a workman, he takes into account not only the man's willingness to labor and his natural capabilities for the task, but also (if he is wise) he considers whether or not there is harmony of thought, purpose, character and vision. If a man's heart is not in his work, his abilities will not be enough in themselves to make him a success.

Many are zealous and eager to serve in the Kingdom, but I cannot use them because their desires and goals are at cross-purposes with Mine.

Luke 14:33

# Purity of motive

Regardless of how sacred may be the nature of a ministry, it may be marred by a heart that is selfish or impure. This is the message of I Corinthians 13. Whatever does not spring out of pure love for God and love for your fellow-man becomes only a hollow noise. All work done for Me in love is thrice blessed, for love is the fulfilling of all the law, and he who labors in love receives understanding.

The work of the Kingdom suffers delay for lack of laborers; but let those who desire to serve, continually offer up a yielded vessel that I may cleanse it from sin and perfect it in righteousness and fill it with love. Only thus is it possible for any man to enter into the activity of the Spirit of God in a way that furthers the divine purpose.

# Adversity

There are no calamities that do not work for your blessing when your heart is directed toward Me. When you do not strive against adversity, its power to hurt you is destroyed. Circumstances may be such that the flesh may suffer, but the spirit will be blessed.

My voice speaks through EVERY situation to the ear that is yielded to the Spirit. My love flows freely through every sorrow to the heart that is devoted to Me. I cannot fail. I will not fail anyone — ever, so long as that one is resting and trusting in My goodness.

Evils pass as ships in the night when peace reigns in the surrendered soul. Leave with Me every unsolved problem. Praise Me, and rejoice while I work it all out for My glory.

I Thess. 5:18

# Health of soul

Never be tolerant of evil. Only with a clear conscience can you minister in power. Others are as aware as you of the health or illness of your soul. Very seldom is any man deceived by another in this regard. You may not know *why* a man is out of fellowship with God, but you do know *that* he is.

Be diligent to maintain an open communication with Me. Let nothing block your prayer channel. Keep your soul exposed to the searchlight of the Holy Spirit, the all-seeing eye of the Father, and the redeeming, cleansing power of the blood of Jesus.

Only then are you a vessel "meet for the Master's use". (II Timothy 2:21)

Psalm 26:2

# The Gethsemane experience

Only through suffering can you be made whole, and the purest joy is in the reflection of the Holy Spirit's work within the soul. I would not have you anticipate continual elation as the norm of a life of faith. I will manifest Myself to you in times of defeat as well as in the hour of exhilaration. Never have I commanded you to pursue happiness as an end in itself. My spirit moves within you to reproduce the character of the Lord Jesus Christ so that your whole personality shall ultimately portray the likeness of the new man. This process is often painful because it entails the annihilation of your own personal will and choices. This was the reason the Lord Jesus Christ sweat as it were drops of blood in the hour of His agony in the Garden of Gethsemane.

The imagination of the natural mind cannot fathom the extent of inner soul struggle through which a man must pass as he undergoes the transforming process of yielding up the natural will to accept the will of the Spirit. That which Holy Scripture reveals of the suffering and passion of the Lord Jesus is in truth a revelation in depth of the very same death struggle which every soul must pass if God's will is chosen in preference to that of the old carnal mind.

I Peter 4:19

# Total relinquishment

As you ponder the sufferings of the Lord Jesus Christ you shall gain insight into your own pain. That which is of the Spirit must be discerned in the Spirit. Only in prayer and meditation on the Holy Word can understanding come to your heart, and only thus can you be truly comforted in the depth of the spirit where the suffering occurs.

Had the disciples remained awake through the bitter hours in the garden, they could have given no help other than prayer. Alone each man undergoes the death throes of his own shattered ego. Nothing can remain of self-will if My full purpose is to be accomplished in the life. Slowly, unrelentingly, each soul moves to his own Gethsamane of total relinquishment of all his cherished personal hopes and on to his own barren Golgotha.

Heb. 4:15

# Submission and redemption

Death is swallowed up in victory only for the man who has committed fully into the hands of the Father his TOTAL being. Be not deceived when confronted by the darkness. Out of the hour of temptation comes the light of My transforming work in your soul. Fear nothing that brings you closer to Me. Be submissive under My hand of discipline. Know that every stroke of the chastening rod effects a further work of redemption.

You have asked to be freed of sin and drawn closer to Me. Trust Me now, as I do My perfecting work in ways you do not understand. You intensify the pain when you question. Trusting reduces spiritual anguish in much the same way that relaxing relieves physical pain.

Lean upon My heart. I take no pleasure in afflicting your soul. I desire always for you a speedy deliverance. You help to bring it as you trust Me and as you yield your soul to whatever instrument I use for the accomplishment of My work in you. (Romans 7:24, 25)

Isa. 48:10

# The Lord is thy life

Fear every voice that calls you to partake of the world. You are IN the world, but not OF it. Keep this distinction clear. Give and take of whatever I bless, but be in bondage to none of its pleasures.

Lasting joy is only in communion with the Heavenly Father. Unmitigated sorrow awaits all who look to the transient entertainment of the world for solace. For all that is in the world, the pleasure of the eyes, the desires of the flesh and the pride of life are emptiness and disappointment. The hunger of the soul is satisfied only by the pure waters from the divine springs. The LORD is thy life. He only is thy salvation.

Psalm 27